Cover illustration: Second Lieutenant Aldwin M. Jucheim climbs into his 78th Fighter Group P-47D Thunderbolt at Duxford, England in early 1944. He is being assisted by his crew chief, S/Sgt. Robert H. McCord. Jucheim would finish the war with ten victories. (US Air Force)

1. Worth fighting for . . . one of the assembly line workers at Lockheed Aircraft puts the finishing touches to a new P-38. With so many of the men in the armed forces, women filled their places to get the United States on a war footing. (Lockheed Aircraft)

2. Training groups of the North American P-51A formed gradually – primarily in the south-east United States – as the type slowly entered the USAAF inventory. During these first operations of the Mustang in group strength, the aircraft's good and bad points were discovered. It was found that, at low level, below 18,000 feet, the P-51A was hard to outrun. (US Air Force)

WARBIRDS ILLUSTRATED NO. 15

American Warplanes

WORLD WAR TWO-KOREA Volume I

Jeffrey L. Ethell

a&ap

ARMS AND ARMOUR PRESS

London—Melbourne—Harrisburg, Pa.

Introduction

Warbird 15: American Warplanes: World War Two – Korea, Vol. I
Published in 1983 by
Arms and Armour Press, Lionel Leventhal Limited, 2–6 Hampstead High Street, London NW3 1QQ; 4–12 Tattersalls Lane, Melbourne, Victoria 3000, Australia; Cameron and Kelker Streets, P.O. Box 1831, Harrisburg, Pennsylvania 17105, USA

British Library Cataloguing in Publication Data:
Ethell, Jeffrey L.
American warplanes: World War Two – Korea. – (Warbirds illustrated series; 15)
Vol. 1
1. United States. (Air Force) – History
2. Airplanes, Military – History
I. Title II. Series
623.74′6′0973 UG1243
ISBN 0-85368-574-6

Layout by Anthony A. Evans.
Printed in Great Britain by William Clowes, Beccles, Limited.

3. Lieutenant William Groseclose boards his 335th Squadron, 4th Fighter Group P-51D at Debden as crew chief S/Sgt. Harry East leans on the drop tank. Most crew chiefs could stand next to their aircraft and catch gremlins by listening. They were more attached to their machines than were the pilots and were the backbone of the USAAF. (US Air Force)

There will most likely never be another period in military aviation quite like the years from 1935 to 1955. Governments around the world prepared for, fought, won and lost wars that accelerated aeronautical research from the biplane era of wood and fabric into the jet age and supersonic flight. Aircraft companies used to measuring a good production run in terms of two digits were called upon to build hundreds, then thousands of warplanes. New designs proliferated, some quite successful and far reaching, others often bizarre. Aeronautical engineers were forced to reach toward ever higher performance in ever shorter time spans.

Within the United States, military aviation was struggling out from under isolationism in the 1930s. Budgets were pitifully small, providing little equipment and even less pay to those required to operate it. Most military planners saw what was coming and tried to prepare, often behind the scenes, but 7 December 1941 still caught America without enough aircraft to fight the Axis powers, and even those machines available were, on the whole, obsolete. But, by 1943, US industrial might was harnessed. The mighty air fleets of 1944 and 1945, launched from both land and sea, were the largest ever assembled. Most likely there will never again be air battles the size of those in the Second World War. By the time the Japanese surrendered, over 300,000 American warplanes had been produced.

Post-war economies led to the scrapping of most of the older piston types, while emphasis was laid on the promise of the jet. The sound barrier was broken and eyes were turned toward space. By 1950 another war had broken out, this time in Korea. Many of the older warbirds, both human and machine, were recalled for duty, resulting in a mixture of the past and present in military aircraft. By 1955 the doors to the space age were opening and manned flight into space would soon be a reality. The soaring costs to perform these feats soon ate into military budgets and an era passed, leaving behind some of the greatest aircraft ever built.

Unless one lived through those years, the impression left is that everything was done in black and white. Colour photography was highly experimental and very little survived. Over the past few years, I have made it a point to collect vintage colour from numerous private, corporate and government sources – the results have been far better than I expected. The reader now has a genuine time capsule in which to travel. The rich variety of military camouflage and markings is difficult to appreciate in art work. Here the aircraft are shown as they were in their natural element, proving to be anything but drab and colourless.

In this first volume, I will trace American military aviation in all services from before Pearl Harbor to after Korea. May you enjoy the trip as much as I have. Without the generosity of those credited on each photograph, this voyage would not have been possible – my deepest thanks for sharing your treasure.

Jeffrey L. Ethell, Richmond, Virginia, 1983.

▲4

▲5 ▼6

4. The primary US Army Air Corps fighter of the late 1930s was the Curtiss P-36 Hawk. These P-36Cs, all of the 27th Pursuit Squadron and wearing 'wargames' camouflage, are lined up at Wright Field, Ohio in September 1939 for the National Air Races.
They were dressed up strictly for Army public relations at the races and the schemes were never used in any wargames or manoeuvres. (US Air Force)
5. A Douglas O-46A attached to the US Army Air Corps' Matériel Division at Wright Field, Ohio in 1940. This was the flight-test headquarters for the Air Corps, where every aircraft purchased for the Army was tested for acceptance or rejection.
Note the Wright Field arrowhead insignia on the side of the fuselage. (NASM Groenhoff Collection)
6. This Boeing B-17C Flying Fortress was attached to the USAAC's Matériel Division in late 1940 for service testing. After one more model change, the B-17 would lose its tall tail to acquire a tail gunner's position. Several B-17Cs and Ds saw action in the early part of the Pacific War and the RAF flew twenty B-17Cs in combat as Fortress Is. (NASM Groenhoff Collection)
7. May 1941, Wright Field, Ohio – Major Stanley Umstead prepares to test fly the Army Air Corp's new Douglas A-20A Havoc (DB-7 Boston in RAF service). The first aircraft, which went to the 3rd Bomb Group, were camouflaged in olive drab and medium green, with neutral grey lower surfaces. The fighter warming up in the background is the first of thirteen Republic YP-43 Lancers delivered to the AAC for testing. (NASM Arnold Collection)
8. RAF export versions of the Bell P-39D reached England by July 1941 as the Airacobra I, eventually flying one mission with No. 601 Squadron in October. Its performance proved to be so poor that the type was dropped from service. The remaining Model 14s were diverted to the Soviets, who found it an excellent ground-attack aircraft. The US Army received many Airacobras built for the British as P-400s, which flew in the Pacific theatre with a mixture of British and US markings.

7▲ 8▼

▲9 ▼10

11▲

9. Grumman F3F-2s of VF-5, USS *Yorktown*, over Pensacola, Florida in about 1939. Though the type flew in first-line service through 1941, it was rapidly replaced by the F4F. This section of aircraft is being led by the squadron commander, as denoted by the full red cowling. The number two aircraft in the unit is flying his left wing (half red upper cowling) and the seventeenth fighter in the squadron (half yellow upper cowling) is flying his right wing. (US Navy)

10. Curtiss was quite successful in building a series of dive-bombers, all named Helldiver. This SBC-4 Helldiver was attached to the New York Naval Reserve in 1941, though most SBCs were attached to the fleet at the time, awaiting replacement by the Douglas SBD. Though still a biplane, the SBC had a metal fuselage, retractable landing gear, enclosed cockpits and a belly rack for either external fuel or a 1,000lb bomb. (NASM Groenhoff Collection)

11. When the US Navy called for a new fighter in late 1935, two companies responded: Brewster and Grumman. Brewster won the competition and the F2A-1 was ordered as the Navy's first monoplane fighter in June 1938. Brewster sold the Buffalo under export to Belgium and Britain as the B-339 during 1939 and 1940. Here, a Belgian Air Force B-339B is test flown in the US, bearing an American registration number on the tail. Only one Buffalo was delivered before Belgium fell and the remaining aircraft were delivered to Britain. (NASM Arnold Collection)

12. The potential of Grumman's Wildcat was proven in testing and, as a result, both the French and British placed orders. By the time the first G-36A was flown in May 1940, France was on the point of capitulation and their order was taken over by the United Kingdom, which christened its new fighter the Martlet I. The second Martlet I is seen here in Fleet Air Arm camouflage, running up at the Grumman Bethpage plant. Arresting gear and folding wings were not added until the Martlet II. (NASM Arnold Collection)

12▼

▲13 ▼14

13. Bell P-39Ds of the 8th Pursuit Group during the 1941 Army manoeuvres in Louisiana. The red crosses were temporary markings for the 'Red Force'. Though excellent performance was obtained from the prototype XP-39, by the time the Airacobra reached Air Corps units it weighed a ton more and had lost quite a bit of speed. It proved a disappointment in combat with the nimble Japanese fighters. (NASM Arnold Collection)
14. A North American BT-9 of the 46th School Squadron in 1941, when the colours true blue and orange-yellow were retained on primary and basic trainers. It was with the BT-9 that the fledgling NAA (North American Aviation) proved itself to both the Army and Navy. Out of this aircraft came the BT-14 and then the AT-6 and SNJ. By July 1942 this classic paint scheme had disappeared from the US Army Air Force (which had been renamed in June 1941) in favour of bare aluminium or camouflage paint. (US Air Force)

15▲ 16▼

15. Curtiss P-40s of the 33rd Pursuit Squadron head up the 8th Pursuit Group line at Langley Field, Virginia in 1941. Though obsolete by the outbreak of the war, the P-40 was the only USAAF fighter available in enough numbers to oppose the Japanese. The American Volunteer Group (Flying Tigers) did quite well against the Japanese in China with their export Hawk 81 versions, known to them simply as P-40s. The RAF used their Tomahawks and later Kittyhawks with skill in North Africa. (US Air Force)
16. The North American O-47 was North American Aviation's first product, built for an Army Air Corps that planned on observation as a major mission. Many O-47s were built for National Guard units relegated to the mission. This O-47B took part in the 1941 manoeuvres as a part of the 'Red Force'. Though the National Guard units were federalized before Pearl Harbor, the O-47 only went to war in a few rare cases. (US Air Force)

▲17

17. An entirely new generation of fighters arrived with Republic's XP-47B Thunderbolt, seen here at the Farmingdale, New York plant. With a 2,000hp Pratt & Whitney engine, the seven-ton prototype easily flew faster than 400mph with a service ceiling of 38,000 feet. The unusual hinged canopy was later replaced by a sliding hood. Though this aircraft crashed in August 1942, the P-47 programme was well advanced. (NASM Arnold Collection)
18. A new generation of heavy bombers was born with the Consolidated XB-24 Liberator, which first flew in December 1939. The initial production batch went to the British as LB-30s (Liberator/British), with deliveries beginning in January 1941. As the war intensified around the world, the US absorbed many of the aircraft destined for British service. This Liberator I was pressed into service with the AAF Ferry Command in November 1941. The RAF camouflage remained and American markings were added along with large US neutrality flags. (US Air Force)
19. By mid-1941 USN fighter squadrons were giving up their F3Fs for Wildcats. VF-5 was no exception; still on the *Yorktown*, they received non-folding wing F3F-3As, pictured here in formation. The Wildcat would fight the war as the Navy's only major fighter until 1943, just as the Army had only the P-40. Though outclassed, these two fighters held the fort in the darkest days of the Pacific War. (NASM Arnold Collection)
20. By the late 1930s the US Coast Guard had a growing fleet of aircraft, used for maritime patrol and search. A number of different types were used in USCG service, such as this brand new Grumman J4F-1 Widgeon on the ramp at the San Francisco Coast Guard Air Station on 18 October 1941. (William T. Larkins)

▼18

19▲ 20▼

▲21

▲22 ▼23

21. With the Japanese attack on Pearl Harbor, 7 December 1941, everyone and everything in the US seemed to be mobilized. This Piper L-4 is warming up for a flight in late 1941, guarded by a soldier with a rifle. The liaison mission would be performed mostly by former civilian aircraft built for the military. (NASM Groenhoff Collection)
22. Many lend-lease aircraft intended for Britain were built alongside machines earmarked for the USAAF inventory, such as this Curtiss P-40E. Its paint scheme pattern is identical to an RAF Kittyhawk IA, but it is painted in Army Air Force medium green and sand with light blue undersurfaces. Though basically inferior in performance to the enemy aircraft it encountered, the P-40 was rugged and had a high diving speed. (NASM Groenhoff Collection)
23. A Stinson O-49 Vigilant stands ready as pilot and observer discuss the forthcoming mission. The Vigilant was later redesignated the L-1. Though its contribution has gone unrecognized, the Vigilant served throughout the war as a liaison and ambulance aircraft. (NASM Groenhoff Collection)
24. By early 1942 the 17th Bomb Group had become operational with the AAF's new North American B-25 Mitchell medium bomber. Crews were delighted with the new aircraft, which was a capable combat aircraft and quite easy to fly. Pictured here is a B-25A with the 34th Squadron of the 17th Group. Note the tail gunner's prone position, which was eliminated on subsequent models. The 17th formed the nucleus for Doolittle's Tokyo Raid in April 1942, using new B-25Bs. (NASM Arnold Collection)
25. A brand new B-17E Flying Fortress for the USAAF during an acceptance test flight. The first of the modern B-17s, the E model had numerous improvements, the most obvious being a new vertical fin and rudder. On 27 September 1941 the first B-17E was delivered. Not until early January 1942 would serial numbers be painted on the tails. Though some of the earlier versions saw combat, it would be this version that initiated the AAF's strategic bombing effort in the Second World War. (US Air Force)

24▲ 25▼

▲26 ▼27

26. In January 1943 the US Navy began to receive its first Grumman F6F-3 Hellcats, which would go into action the following August. This 2,000hp brute turned out to be one of the easiest to fly of all the Second World War fighters. It was stable, controllable below stall speed, faster than the Zero, and a fine gun platform. Pilots found it a great improvement over the F4F. (NASM Groenhoff Collection)

27. Another new arrival for the US Navy in 1942, Grumman's TBF-1 Avenger torpedo-bomber. The first example was delivered in January and the type was in action with VT-8 in the Battle of Midway in June. The Avenger became the Navy's major torpedo-bomber of the Second World War. (NASM Groenhoff Collection)

28. An F6F-3 from VF-5 comes aboard the USS *Yorktown* (CV-10) in May 1943 during the new carrier's shakedown cruise. 'Fighting Five' was the first Navy squadron to take the Hellcat into combat, on 31 August 1943 against Marcus Island. (US Navy)

29. A brand new F6F-3 with the landing gear down during slow speed practice, photographed over Treasure Island, near San Francisco in October 1942. With its big wing, the Hellcat proved to be quite stable at low speeds, making it just about perfect for carrier landings, which it could achieve at a speed 5mph slower than the F4F. After about twelve field landings, pilots found themselves well qualified to bring the fighter aboard ship for the first time. Note the early blue-grey/light grey scheme and the tape over the gun ports. (US Navy)

30. The great primary trainer of the Second World War was Boeing's Stearman Kaydet. This is the Navy's N2S-2 version with a fixed pitch wooden prop and a hand crank inertia starter. The Kaydet was known as the PT-13 and PT-17 in the USAAF, and along with the N3N was nicknamed the 'Yellow Peril' due to the student chrome yellow paint scheme. This particular Stearman is an instrument trainer (red bands) attached to the Corpus Christi, Texas (blue rudder) area in about 1942. (NASM Groenhoff Collection)

28▲

29▲ 30▼

▲31 ▼32

31. By the end of July 1942 the Navy was taking delivery of the Vought F4U-1 Corsair which, during October 1940, had become the first US fighter of any type to exceed 400mph. Though ordered and flown long before the F6F, the Corsair had a number of teething problems that kept it from entering service before late 1942, and then as a land-based aircraft. This early F4U-1 has the old-style braced canopy, which was later replaced with a bubble hood and a higher seat for improved visibility over the long nose. (NASM Arnold Collection)

32. Though the Navy was not ready to base its Corsairs aboard carriers when initial deliveries were made, the British Royal Navy did not hesitate to take the aircraft on lend-lease as Corsair F Mk. Is from early 1943. The Fleet Air Arm located aircrew training at US Naval Air Stations Quonset Point and Brunswick. When a complete squadron was ready, it was shipped to the UK on an escort carrier, ready for action. The first such unit was No. 1830 Squadron, commissioned on 1 June 1943 and then attached to HMS *Illustrious.* (US Navy)

33. 20 March 1943 – Air Group Nine aboard the new aircraft carrier USS *Essex*, heading for action in the Pacific. The new F6F-3 Wildcats of VF-9 had not seen combat when this photograph was taken. The SBD Dauntlesses of VB-9 would join their big fighter brothers in combat over Marcus Island on 1 September 1943. As is obvious, spotting aircraft on a carrier deck was like working out a gigantic jigsaw puzzle. (US Navy)

33▼

▲34

34. A brand new A-20C Havoc runs up at the Douglas plant in southern California in about mid-1942. Known as the Boston III in the RAF, the majority of this version of the effective attack bomber were given under lend-lease to Britain and the Soviet Union. (US Air Force)

35. A Douglas P-70A (top) escorted by a Bell P-39N and a North American P-51A (foreground). In late 1942 these were the Army Air Force's new fighters. Though the P-70 night fighter was converted from the A-20 as an interim step until the arrival of the P-61 Black Widow, it did see limited action in the Pacific. The Allison-engined P-51A entered combat the next year and was well received by its pilots. (US Air Force)

36. Barbara Jane Erickson (in the cockpit) and Evelyn Sharp of the 6th Ferry Group, Women's Auxiliary Ferrying Squadron (WAFS) with an early P-51A; Long Beach, California, early 1943. As the war went on, the number of women pilots assigned to ferry first-line combat aircraft grew until the Women's Airforce Service Pilots (WASPs) were formed in July 1943. Evelyn Sharp was later killed in the crash of her P-38, while Barbara Erickson survived the war to win an Air Medal. (US Air Force)

37. A P-38H Lightning on the line at Lockheed's Burbank, California facility, ready for acceptance testing. The factory-fresh paint would not last long once the fighter was flying with an Army squadron. (Lockheed Aircraft)

▼35

36▲ 37▼

▲38

▲39 ▼40

38. A formation of Curtiss AT-9 Fledgling (better known as the Jeep) advanced twin-engine trainers. This bulbous aircraft was known as one of the hottest of the advanced trainers, since it was challenging to land and a bear to handle on one engine. In many ways it was hotter than the bombers and transports in front-line service, providing excellent training for the would-be pilot of multi-engine aircraft. (US Air Force)

39. The USAAF formed several transition units with obsolete bombers and fighters in order to give recently graduated cadets first-hand experience with operational types. This early model P-40 was assigned to Luke Field, Arizona to give would-be fighter pilots their first taste of the real thing. (US Air Force)

40. A very real part of the US war effort involved Hollywood. One of the better films made concerning the USAAF was 'Air Force', starring John Garfield, which followed the fortunes of a single B-17 crew from its flying into the attack on Pearl Harbor to the invasion of Wake Island. The realism and lack of propaganda were enhanced by the crew's B-17C, named 'Mary Ann', seen here on 6 April 1943 when it was placed back into training command. (US Air Force)

41. After Pearl Harbor there was concern that the Axis would hit the Panama Canal and block the flow of supplies to the Pacific. Though the attack never took place, several fighter and bomber groups were stationed in the Canal Zone. This P-39Q of the 53rd Fighter Group is undergoing maintenance at Madden Field, Panama. (US Air Force)

42. The first Lightnings to enter combat were P-38Es of the 54th Fighter Squadron, which began sorties against the Japanese in the Aleutians on 3 September 1942. This 54th Squadron P-38E is undergoing a gear retraction test at the 11th Air Force base of Adak in late 1942. The weather proved to be the main enemy in the frozen north. (US Air Force)

41▲ 42▼

▲43 ▼44 ▼45

46▲

43. The rugged Republic Thunderbolt quickly made a name for itself in combat, despite its seven-ton bulk. With light ailerons, it had a roll rate faster than the Spitfire and tremendous firepower with eight .50 calibre guns. This P-47D is assigned to a stateside training unit. (US Air Force)

44. B-17Fs of the 401st Squadron, 91st Bombardment Group fly low over England in early 1943. The 91st, based at Bassingbourne, was one of the pioneer 8th Air Force heavy bomb groups. It was the first group to attack a target in the Ruhr–Hamm on 4 March 1943. (US Air Force)

45. The 14th Fighter Group's ground echelon moves from Tunisia to Italy aboard C-47s, painted in what would later be known as invasion stripes; late 1943. Although protected by the Group's Lightnings, the 'Gooney Birds' were still defenceless and these long trips were sweated out by all aboard. (Ira LaTour)

46. June 1943 brought a major insignia change for the United States: bars were added to the round star and blue background, with a red border surrounding the entire marking. This colourful system lasted only a few months, and was replaced by a blue surround as it was confused at a distance with the Japanese red hinomaru insignia. This P-40K provides a good view of the new marking. Though the removal of the red was ordered in August 1943, examples could often be found well into 1944. (US Air Force)

47. Brand new JRF-5 Goose amphibians on the line at Grumman Aircraft on Long Island in July 1943. An acceptance test pilot is being dropped off by one of the many small scooters the company used for transportation around the large airfield. The other scooter contains auxiliary power and compressed gas bottles to get the aircraft serviced and started. (NASM Arnold Collection)

47▼

48. Captain Willie Haning of the newly formed 475th Fighter Group at Ipswich, near Brisbane in August 1943. The 475th was the only new group in the 5th Air Force to form outside the US, such was the need for saving time in getting more P-38s into combat. Note the marks where tape was applied on all seams for shipment of the fighter across the Pacific. The sealant hopelessly marred the olive drab and grey paint. (Dennis Glenn Cooper)

49. The dawn of the jet age for the United States in the late summer of 1943. Here, a Bell YP-59A Airacomet flies near the USAAF test area at Muroc AAB, California, now Edwards AFB. The first flight of the XP-59A in October 1942 came well after the German and British first jet flights. America's first jet had barely the performance of contemporary propeller-driven types, but it was a start. (US Air Force)

▲48 ▼49

50. Though virtually obsolete before Pearl Harbor, the 'Slow But Deadly' Dauntless served effectively to the end of the war. The type took part in all five naval engagements fought exclusively by aircraft carriers, and sank more enemy carriers (6) than any other aircraft. Over 300,000 tons of enemy shipping went down under the SBD, including the three Japanese carriers sunk at the Battle of Midway. Here, three Dauntlesses patrol the Pacific in 1944. (US Navy)

51. Vought's V-173 Flapjack was certainly one of the most unusual aircraft to appear during the Second World War. Enough interest was shown in the circular wing concept for the F5U advanced version with retractable landing gear to be ordered, but although two were built they were never flown. The V-173 flew many times, initially on 23 November 1942. (NASM Arnold Collection)

50▲ 51▼

▲52 ▼53

52. The P-38J of Warren G. Campbell, 94th Squadron, 1st Fighter Group, Foggia, Italy. 'Old Rusty', as his aircraft was named, carried Campbell through 43 missions in the Mediterranean theatre, where twin-engine reliability made the Lightning a much-loved fighter. (Warren Campbell)
53. An F-5A Lightning of the 3rd Photo Reconnaissance Group in Italy, 1944. The synthetic haze blue paint was quite distinctive. The effect at altitude was to make the Lightning basically invisible until very close range, since the colour blended in quite well with the high-altitude colour of the sky. On solo recce flights without armament, this was extremely important in avoiding enemy fighters. (via Dana Bell)
54. Mud, mud, mud – Foggia, Italy during the spring thaw in 1944. Lightning maintenance was never easy, but the weather often made it close to impossible. Work stands would sink into the mud and aircraft would be bogged down into the gumbo that swallowed things forever. These 48th Fighter Squadron mechanics are working on a P-38J. (Ira LaTour)
55. In spite of the mud, Italy could often be beautiful. A 48th Fighter Squadron P-38J, No. 13, taxies out at Foggia into a beautiful sunrise, 1944. (Ira LaTour)
56. The cockpit of P-38J-10-LO, 42-67762; on the left are the red-topped throttles, prop pitch controls and mixture controls. Behind the control yoke in the centre is the main switch box and armament selectors with the magneto switches on the upper left. The machine-gun and cannon triggers are on the wheel handles, while the red dive flap switch is on the left brace and the white microphone button is on the right brace. The printed placards on the yoke are dive limiting speeds (left) and power and flap settings (right). The flap handle is just to the right of the yoke, mounted on the left side of the cockpit just in front of the radio and light controls. Oxygen regulator and controls are mounted on the centre floor between the rudder pedals.

54▲

55▲ 56▼

▲57 ▼58

57. An Interstate TDR-3 at the Naval Air Modification Unit, NAS Johnsville, Pennsylvania. This aircraft was developed to be a pilotless, remote-controlled bomb with an RCA television camera in the nose. After being tested with a pilot aboard, NOLO or pilotless flights were successful and, eventually, an operational unit was formed in New Guinea. Successful bombing attacks with the TDRs were made against Rabaul before the war ended. (NASM Arnold Collection)

58. P-47s of the 56th Fighter Group getting ready to stage out of their 8th Air Force field at Boxted, England in 1944. The 56th produced more aces than any other USAAF group in the Second World War, running up a score of over 1,000 enemy aircraft destroyed. Though other groups in the 8th exchanged their Thunderbolts for Mustangs, the 56th stayed with their faithful mount for all 447 combat missions. (via William Hess)

59. B-26 Marauders of the 495th Squadron, 344th Bomb Group line up for take-off to Cologne from their 9th Air Force base at Cormeilles-en-Vexin, France. Before moving in at Cormeilles the Group had bombed this base when it was in Luftwaffe hands. By this point in the war only olive drab was being field-applied to the shiny new Marauders; on the aircraft illustrated, grey paint covers what is left of the invasion stripes below the wings and fuselage. (via Garry Fry)

60. Lieutenant John H. Meyers with his 386th Bomb Group Marauder 'La Paloma'. Regarded as a dangerous aircraft when it first came out, the B-26 ended up with fewer losses per mission than any other USAAF type. (NASM/John H. Meyers)

59▲ 60▼

◀61

62▲

61. The legendary leader of the 8th Air Force's 4th Fighter Group, Colonel Don Blakeslee, at Debden, England in mid-1944. A demanding leader, he had the ability to grasp the entirety of a combat situation and deploy his fighters wisely. (US Air Force)

62. Lieutenant James Fisk examines flak damage to his 52nd Fighter Group Mustang in Italy. The flak round came right through the ammunition storage bays, a good reason for Fisk to cross his fingers for good luck. (US Air Force)

63. Major Sam Brown was an ace with the 307th Squadron of the 31st Fighter Group, 15th Air Force in Italy. Over Vienna on 26 June 1944, Brown claimed four destroyed and two probables. The flare pistol port just above the last two kill markings has been sealed over; flares were rarely used in the air. On most of the occasions when a pilot had to use them, he was down and in need of rescue. (US Air Force)

63▼

▲64

64. A 58th Fighter Group P-47D on the way back from a mission to Santiago, North Luzon, Philippines late in the war. Assigned primarily to ground support, the 58th was the only group in the south-west Pacific area still flying Thunderbolts when the war ended. (US Air Force)

65. P-47Ds of 1 Grupo de Aviacão de Caca, Forca Aerea Brasileira (1st Fighter Group, Brazilian Air Force) attached to the 350th Fighter Group, 12th Air Force, Pisa, Italy. The Brazilians were quite active in combat for the last six months of the war in the Mediterranean. (US Air Force)

66. A Northrop P-61A Black Widow of the 425th Night Fighter Squadron, 9th Air Force, France, late 1944. The first American fighter designed specifically for night fighting, the P-61 did its job well. With spoilers on the wings for roll control, it proved quite manoeuvrable for its size, and its firepower of four .50 calibre and four 20mm cannon was murderous. (US Air Force)

67. B-17Gs of the 381st Bomb Group, escorted by a P-51B of the 355th Fighter Group, on a practice mission over England in late summer 1944. At first its crews feared that the loss of olive drab and grey paint for a shiny natural metal finish would attract enemy fighters, but at altitude the bare aluminium proved harder to spot. (US Air Force)

▼65

66▲ 67▼

▲68

▲69 ▼70

71▲

68. With the end of the Second World War came occupation of the conquered countries. Here, Jacques Young, 3rd Squadron, 3rd Air Commando Group, flies his 'Jumpin Jacques' over Japan in September 1945 while based at Chitose. (Jacques Young)
69. Second Lieutenant Marvin W. Arthur's 'Davy Lee' at Debden, England in March 1945. In the European theatre it was usual for aircraft to be handed on. The P-51 Mustang shown here used to be Clarence Boretsky's QP-B, 'Meg', though it did remain in the 4th Fighter Group's 334th Squadron. (via Garry Fry)
70. Mustangs of the 3rd Air Commando Group at their base; Chitose, Japan in 1946. When the Group finally went home, their P-51s were turned over to P-38 pilots who would carry on the occupation. In short order several were wrecked as the twin-engine pilots again became familiar with a powerful single-engine fighter. (Don Maggert)
71. The USAAF ordered 900 Curtiss SB2C Helldivers as A-25As, though most of the run went to the Marine Corps as SB2C-1As. Used primarily for training in the States, the A-25 towed targets and performed mundane tasks as a hack aircraft. The nickname 'Torchy Tess' on this A-25 recalls the unpleasant susceptibility of the early A-25s to engine fires. The big dive-bomber was not a favourite aircraft among most Army pilots. (NASM Groenhoff Collection)
72. 'Flak Bait': this 9th Air Force B-26B Marauder, assigned to the 449th Squadron of the 322nd Bomb Group, flew 202 missions from the time it entered combat in the summer of 1943 to the end of the war in April 1945. Few if any aircraft, and certainly no other American bomber, equalled the record. In spite of the Martin's ability to absorb continual combat damage, crews felt the name 'Flak Bait' was particularly appropriate since the ship attracted flak like a magnet. (C. F. McClain)

72▼

▲73

▲74 ▼75

76▲

73. The Culver PQ-14A was manufactured for the USAAF as a radio-controlled target drone that could also be manned and flown by a pilot. Of the 1,348 examples built, 1,201 were transferred to the USN as TD2C-1s. Target drones were found to be quite effective in teaching both air-to-air and air-to-ground gunnery, and the concept has survived to the present day. (W. J. Balogh, Sr., via Dave Menard)

74. Though the Bell Airacomet was outclassed by its contemporary piston-engined stable-mates, it was ordered into production to give experience with jet-propelled types. Of the 20 P-59As and 30 P-59Bs built, most went to equip the 412th Fighter Group, which had formed as the USAAF's first jet fighter unit at Muroc in November 1943 before moving to Bakersfield then Santa Maria, California by July 1945. This P-59B was spotted at Corapolis AAF, Pennsylvania in 1945. (Dave Menard)

75. Though not very glamorous, utility aircraft served the AAF well in performing mundane chores. This shop-worn Noorduyn UC-64A Norseman (43-5124) stands ready for duty in August 1946. It was in this type of aircraft that famous band-leader Glenn Miller was lost while flying out of England in 1944. (W. J. Balogh, Sr., via Dave Menard)

76. The post-war AAF wound down in both numbers of personnel and pilots, with several aircraft types being singled out as standard equipment while the remainder were either sold or scrapped. The Douglas A-26 Invader had the performance and versatility to remain in the active inventory through the 1950s, redesignated the B-26 after the Martin Marauder was stricken from service. (Picciani Aircraft Slides)

77. Black Widows saw much post-war service in the Far East Air Forces and in the United States. By June 1948 all P designations were done away with after the US Air Force had been officially formed as an independent service the previous year – thus the F-61 soldiered on into the late 1940s. This P-61B was at Corapolis AAF, Pennsylvania in 1945. (W. J. Balogh, Sr., via Dave Menard)

77▼

▼78 ▲79

78. Occupation was a way of life, often of longer duration than many wanted. Here, George McWilliams flies a P-47D of the 397th Squadron, 368th Fighter Group over the Bavarian Alps in the autumn of 1946. The Group, along with the 404th Fighter Group, was based at Straubing, Germany. (Arthur Houston)

79. F-47Ds of the 527th Squadron, 86th Fighter Group, the last US Air Force Thunderbolt group stationed in Europe during the late 1940s on dispersal at Celle, Germany in 1948. Once a few Air National Guard squadrons had finished flying the big fighter, it disappeared almost without trace. (Colonel R. C. Casey via Dave Menard)

80. Squadrons of the 86th Fighter Group while flying F-47Ds in Europe, c. 1949–50. The 'Jug' certainly went out in a blaze of glory. (Colonel G. A. Larson via Dave Menard)

80▲

▲81

81. Ever larger piston-engined aircraft emerged from the design tables of the early 1940s, dwarfing contemporaries by the last years of the decade. Among the more successful examples was the Douglas C-74A, seen here at Westover AFB, Massachusetts in February 1947. The pilots had individual 'bug eye' canopies, later done away with in favour of a single flight deck when the design evolved into the C-124. (W. J. Balogh, Sr., via Dave Menard)

82. An A-26 of the 3rd Bomb Group, Yokota, Japan in early 1947, still in the olive drab paint carried when the unit was in combat over the Pacific with the 5th Air Force. A spare bare metal cowling has been installed on No. 1 engine and the olive drab paint on the rudder looks characteristically lighter green as it did when applied to doped fabric. (Colonel Underhill via Dave Menard)

83, 84. One of the most famous aircraft ever built, the Bell XS-1, on 14 October 1947, the day Charles Yeager flew it to become the first man to break the sound barrier. Shaped like a bullet, the rocket-powered research aircraft was the first in a long line of X-series machines that would probe the limits of technology in order to push man farther, faster and higher. (Charles Yeager via NASM)

▼82

83▲ 84▼

▲85

▲86 ▼87

88▲

85. F-51Ds over Mount Ranier, Washington in about 1948 when the 'enemy' most sought after was the Navy's F8F Bearcat. Mustang pilots had to admit that the tiny Grumman was a formidable foe, generally faster and more manoeuvrable, when pilots would bounce each other for mock dogfights. (Don Maggert)
86. The North American P-82 Twin Mustang was a development of the XP-51F lightweight fighter, leading to the P-51H. The concept was for a long-range bomber escort with two pilots, but the war ended before the 'Double-Breasted Mustang' could see action. However, the USAF's new Strategic Air Command saw it as an all-weather fighter as well as an escort for the new B-50. These P-82Es belonged to SAC's 27th Fighter Group, Kearney AFB, Nebraska. (Don Maggert)
87. An F-51D piloted by Harry White of the 39th Squadron, 35th Fighter Group, Japan, in 1949 just after he had made an emergency landing. White had been forced down after losing most of his oil, the majority of which had come out of the small breather port under the letter R. (via Bob Esposito)
88. An early P-80A turned into a drone at Wright Field, Ohio. The Shooting Stars were flown in pairs, one drone and its controller, during these tests in the 1940s. Earlier jet drone/controller flight tests had been carried out with P-59As and Bs before using the P-80. (via Dave Menard)
89. Second World War ace Colonel David Schilling's P-80A, 62nd Squadron, 56th Fighter Group at the National Air Races in September 1947. Schilling's 23 victory symbols have been painted just under the rear of the canopy, denoting the German aircraft he downed while flying P-47s with the 56th out of England. Note the P-63 racer taxiing in the background at left. (via Dave Menard)

89▼

▲90 ▼91

92▲

90. When Air National Guard units began to get the F-51H as it was phased out of the USAF inventory, pilots were universally impressed with the hot-rod performance of this lightweight Mustang. The Maryland ANG flew them extensively, at one time putting up a four aircraft aerobatic team known as the 'Guardian Angels'. (Picciani Aircraft Slides)

91. The B-26 flew well into the 1950s as a major USAF medium bomber. These 126th Bomb Group Invaders are on the line outside Bordeaux, France in April 1952. There is a mixture of both solid and glass-nosed aircraft, as was the case in most Invader units of the period. (Fred Justice, Jr.)

92. An F-51H attached to the 101st Squadron, 102nd Fighter Group, Massachusetts ANG at Boston. Reflecting the ethnic backgrounds of the local pilots, the unit's two squadrons were known as the 'Irish Squadron' and the 'Polish Squadron'. Flying with the Guard was always great fun. (Picciani Aircraft Slides)

▲93

93. North American's AT-6 trainer seemed to last and last. In the early 1950s, examples were remanufactured as the T-6G and new Harvard IVs were being built in Canada. Air National Guard units found great use for Texans, since Mustangs predominated as the regular Air Force received jets. A T-6 check-out was virtually mandatory before flying the Mustang. This T-6G with the Michigan ANG warms up for a check flight. (W. J. Balogh, Sr., via Dave Menard)

94. Late August 1952: the 192nd Fighter Bomber Squadron, 131st Group, George AFB, California just before the last overseas deployment of active USAF Mustangs. Most of the aircraft have already been painted with arctic red markings, appropriate for their destination – Iceland. FF-197 remains in the colourful markings of the squadron commander, Major E. C. Ethell, the author's father, who led this deployment of 35 F-51s. (Airchive via Dave McLaren)

95. Many ANG units were assigned F-47s as one era gave way to another. Here, Ed Bollen of the Pennsylvania ANG gets ready for a mission in his F-47D. The soft helmet has given way to the hard hat or 'brain bucket', but normal issue sunglasses were still required since dark visors had not yet been developed for the new jet jockey helmets. (Ed Bollen)

▼94

95▶

STEP

▲96

96. By the early 1950s the jet age was firmly established as American military units continued the transition from the outmoded propeller-driven types. These Republic F-84E Thunderjets of the 23rd Squadron, 36th Fighter Bomber Group formed part of the US presence in Europe at Furstenfeldbruck, February 1952. (Fred Justice, Jr., via Dave Menard)

97. Many of the obsolete piston-engined aircraft were converted to drones, such as this F6F-5K on the east coast in 1952. Hellcat drones served as targets, research vehicles and training aircraft, with most ending up totally destroyed or on the scrap heap. (W. J. Balogh, Sr., via Dave Menard)

98. The reliable Consolidated PBY Catalina saw extensive service from before the Second World War through the 1950s, even though it was very slow. Built under contract by Canadian Vickers and the Naval Aircraft Factory as the OA-10A and B, it was supplied to the USAAF during the war as a patrol and rescue aircraft. This USAF OA-10A was still serving with the USAF in the early 1950s as air/sea-rescue amphibian par excellence. It was replaced by the Grumman SA-16. (US Air Force)

99. This VU-4 F7F-2D Tigercat served as the drone controller for the Hellcat in photograph 97. The drone pilot would sit in the rear cockpit to fly the F6F; note that the canopy and windshield are stock F8F Bearcat parts, as were many items in the rear seat. (W. J. Balogh, Sr., via Dave Menard)

▼97

98▲ 99▼

▲100 ▼101

100. An F8F-1 Bearcat coming aboard the USS *Monterey* in March 1951. The tiny Grumman was near the apex in piston-engined fighters, universally loved by pilots for its manoeuvrability and performance. The 'Bear' remained in the USN inventory into the 1950s as a fighter transition and currency aircraft. By the middle of the decade, they were phased out in favour of jets. (E. W. Quandt via Dave Menard)
101. The major USN fighter of the 1950s was the Grumman F9F. This Marine F9F-5P Panther was attached to VMJ-3 at MCAS Miami, Florida as a photo-reconnaissance aircraft. The next F9F, the -6, had swept wings and was called the Cougar. (W. J. Balogh, Sr., via Dave Menard)
102. Though operated primarily by the US Army, the de Havilland L-20 Beaver served other services quite well as a utility and liaison aircraft while attached to various units and commands. This L-20A served with the USAF 461st Bomb Wing in about 1954. (W. J. Balogh, Sr., via Dave Menard)
103. Another Second World War veteran that lasted far longer than expected was the Douglas C-47, commonly referred to as the 'Gooney Bird' by its crews. Though relegated for the most part to transportation duties, as this Military Air Transport Service C-47D, it was placed back into combat as a gunship during the Vietnam War. (W. J. Balogh, Sr., via Dave Menard)
104. The mammoth Douglas C-124 Globemaster was the USAF's first step into heavy airlift on a regular basis. The aircraft had numerous decks and, at the time, an almost limitless capacity. It was the last of the over-sized piston-engined transports. This C-124 had just made an emergency landing at Johnston Island in the middle of the Pacific Ocean after being accidentally refuelled with JP-4 jet fuel – it barely made it back. (Richard Goold via Dave McLaren)

102▲

103▲ 104▼

▲105

105. This 68th Fighter (All Weather) Squadron F-82G Twin Mustang, 'Bucket of Bolts', made the first kill of the Korean War on 27 June 1950. Lieutenant William Hudson and Lieutenant Carl Fraser downed a Yak-7U out of a flight of five attempting to strafe Kimpo Airfield. Two more Yaks were downed by F-82s that day and another war was on. (B. C. Reed via Dave McLaren)

106. Another 68th Squadron Twin Mustang on take-off from Tague for a combat sortie in 1951. Though primarily a night fighter, the F-82G was used extensively during daylight hours. (via Dave Menard)

▼106

107▲

107. Preparing a No. 77 Squadron, RAAF, F-51D for combat at the 35th Fighter Group's base in Korea. Napalm, or jellied gasoline, was pumped into the large drop tanks on the bomb racks, then an ignitor fuze was attached. (Gerald Brown)
108. A 12th Squadron, 18th Fighter Bomber Group F-51D is flagged off from Chinhae, loaded with 500lb bombs. Though losses were often heavy, the Mustang performed the close air support and ResCap roles well due to its ability to loiter in the target area far longer than jets. (US Air Force)
109. (overleaf) Walk around – pilots of the 45th Tactical Reconnaissance Squadron give their RF-51Ds a pre-flight check before a mission over Korea. Armed reconnaissance was a job well suited to the Mustang, in spite of the vulnerability of its liquid-cooled engine, since the cameras in the rear fuselage provided hard evidence of potential targets and strike results. (US Air Force)

108▼

My Mimi

U.S. AIR FORCE

▲110 ▼111

112▲

110. Mustangs from three squadrons, the 12th, 39th and 67th, can be seen warming up at Chinhae prior to a sortie. Massive strikes such as these were reminiscent of the Second World War, although it was an entirely different war fought under different rules. (US Air Force)
111. The T-6/SNJ also made a return to first-line combat in the Korean War, this time as the LT-6G with USAF Mosquito forward air control aircraft. This SNJ belonged to the Joint Operations Center – Korea in 1951 as a liaison aircraft. (Reiling via Larry Davis)

112. Just about every aircraft type showed up in Korea if a use could be found for it. The Ryan (formerly North American) L-17 Navion served as a utility transport and all-purpose aircraft, appearing at several front-line bases. This L-17B was attached to the US Army. (Charles N. Trask via Dave McLaren)
113. The graceful lines of Lockheed's Constellation, seen here as a C-121C with Military Air Transport Service, made it one of the more popular aircraft of the era, both militarily and commercially. During the Korean War, it hauled all manner of supplies across the Pacific. (Charles N. Trask via Dave McLaren)

113▼

▲114 ▼115

116▲

114. With Korea came the first jet vs jet war, with the North American F-86 and the MiG-15 being the major opponents. Another batch of aces resulted, with the kill ratio in favour of the Sabre by about 7:1. These F-86Es of the 67th Squadron, 18th Fighter Bomber Wing at Tague are seen enduring typically poor weather. (Dave McLaren)

115. 'Nina II' was flown by Colonel John Mitchell, commander of 51st Fighter Interceptor Wing, who downed two MiGs. Pierced steel planking was the rule of the day for airfields in Korea. This surface could be very treacherous, particularly if a jagged piece of steel punctured a tyre or if it was slippery, as was often the case. (US Air Force)

116. Sabres of the 334th Squadron, 4th Fighter Interceptor Group on patrol high over Korea. The 4th emerged as the top-scoring unit of the war, just as it had in the Second World War. Though the MiG-15 was superior to the F-86 in many ways, the Sabre's rate of roll and quality of pilot was consistently superior. (Vernon Hesterman)

▲117

117. This Douglas AD-3 Skyraider, Bu.No.122729, is seen here patrolling off Korea in 1950. Skyraider production did not end until February 1957. This aircraft is carrying an electronics countermeasures (ECM) radar pod under the left wing with a radar operator's cockpit in the fuselage behind the pilot. Both the N and Q models were fitted in this manner. The four stripes on the leading edge of the vertical stabilizer aided the Landing Signal Officer in judging carrier approaches. (Larry Davis via Dave Menard)

118. Yet another ghost from a previous war fights again, and quite effectively – a VMA-323 Corsair at Chin Chan in 1952. (Picciani Aircraft Slides)

119. September 1952 – USS *Boxer* (CV-21) prepares to use the old Hellcat in combat again, only this time as a radio-controlled guided missile in Korean waters. The AD-1 mother ship is warming up alongside. (US Navy)

▼118 119▶

NAVY
15

▲120

120. A Marine AU-1 Corsair, a specially built version of the F4U-5, of VMA-323 at Chin Chan, 1952. Close air support with the Corsair, from both USMC and USN squadrons, was very welcome and accurate. As with the other prop-driven aircraft, long loiter time and heavy firepower were the Corsair's strong points. (Picciani Aircraft Slides)

▼121

121. A Marine McDonnell F2H-2P Banshee attached to VMJ-1 at Tague for photographic-reconnaissance work. Along with the Grumman Panther, the 'Banjo' and its predecessor the FH-1 Phantom took the Navy into the jet age just in time for the Korean War. (Petrie via Dave McLaren)